This book is to be returned on or before
the last date stamped below.

Calcutta under a pall of smoke after the Direct Action Day riots. The buildings have been looted and burnt.

THE
PARTITION
OF INDIA

V. P. (Hemant) Kanitkar

The Arab-Israeli Issue
The Conflict in Afghanistan
The Division of Berlin
The Cuban Missile Crisis
The Hungarian Uprising
The Partition of India
The Irish Question
The Revolution in Iran
The Korean War
The Crisis in South Africa
The Suez Crisis
The Vietnam War

First published in 1987 by
Wayland (Publishers) Ltd
61 Western Road, Hove
East Sussex BN3 1JD, England

British Library Cataloguing in Publication Data

Kanitkar, V.P.
   The partition of India. – (Flashpoints).
   1. India – Politics and government –
   1919–1947
   I. Title   II. Series
   945.03'59   DS480.83
   54
   ISBN 1–85210–023–0

Phototypeset by Kalligraphics Ltd, Redhill, Surrey
Printed and bound in the UK by The Bath Press, Avon

Contents

1 Direct Action Day   8
2 Religious forces   12
3 The Three-Nation Contest   18
4 'Divide and Quit'   32
5 Towards a 'moth-eaten' Pakistan   37
6 The transfer of power   47
7 The immediate aftermath   51
8 The legacy: India   59
9 The legacy: Pakistan   65
   Date chart   73
   Glossary   75
   Further reading   76
   Index   77

1

Direct Action Day

A Calcutta street littered with corpses. The anti-Hindu riots in August 1946 left about 4 000 people dead and 11 000 wounded.

The events of 16 August 1946 helped to change the course of Indian history. On that morning, as the grey mist was lifted by the first rays of the sun, small groups of hired thugs, called *goondas*, crossed the river into the city of Calcutta. They were armed with bamboo sticks, iron bars, bottles and knives.

Muhammad Ali Jinnah, leader of the Muslim League, had announced that this was to be Direct Action Day, during which Muslims throughout India would reaffirm their desire to have their own separate country: Pakistan. All Muslim shops were shut in support of the *hartal* (non-violent boycott) declared by the Muslim League. Local Muslim leaders, however, were prepared to use any methods to attack the Hindus. These *goondas* were from the city slums and they were ready to stab or beat any unwary Hindu shopkeepers who opened their stores for business.

When Hindu shops began to open, the owners were stabbed or beaten with sticks; then the shops were looted, furniture and fittings smashed, glass shattered. Street sweepers were clubbed and, as they fell to the ground, their throats were slit. Old men and women were pushed, kicked and clubbed until they lay bleeding in the gutter.

Muhammad Ali Jinnah (right), leader of the Muslim League, who called for Direct Action Day as part of the campaign for a separate Muslim state.

The violence spreads

All morning the thugs looted and set shops alight. The police looked on but did nothing, and at first very few people realized that the violence had been pre-arranged. The *goondas* were joined by onlookers who now began to kill as well. The rioting spread quickly. By the afternoon, Hindus and Sikhs came out in large numbers for revenge and reprisal. All over Calcutta communal violence flared, but the states of Punjab and Sind in the north-west of India (areas where Muslims were in the majority) remained quiet. In Bombay, a Hindu majority area, black flags flew from Muslim houses, but there was no rioting.

On the second day the army was called upon to deal with the riots. When the troops appeared, the *goondas* fled. On the surface everything appeared to be under control, but the stabbings and clubbings went on in the alleyways. In forty-eight hours over 5,000 people died in Calcutta. These communal riots later spread to Noakhali, Bihar and the Punjab. The killings continued even after partition, when the separate Muslim state of Pakistan had been created. In all, nearly half a million Hindu, Muslim and Sikh lives were lost.

Rioting between Muslims and Hindus spreads. The house of a rich Hindu banker, looted and destroyed by rioters, at Cawnpore.

The political background

What was the trigger for this violence and religious tension between Muslims and Hindus in the India of 1946?

For many years, India had been part of the British Empire. Now, the British government had finally put forward a plan to enable India to become independent. At first this plan had been accepted by both the Indian Congress Party and by the Muslim League, but later the League withdrew its support. The great hope of Mahatma Gandhi, and of many others, had been that India could become independent as one whole, united country. But religious tensions were too great. The Muslim League pressed for a Muslim state, Pakistan, to be created, quite separate from the Hindu majority of India.

Gandhi's dream of a united India was not to be. On the first day of the 1946 riots, the head of the Muslim government in Bengal, Mr. Shaheed Suhrawardy, addressed a public meeting, thanking Muslim League members for their active work for the establishment of Pakistan.

The Calcutta killings had demonstrated that power could not be transferred to a United India, because it appeared that Hindus and Muslims could not live peaceably together. The partition of India appeared to loom ever nearer.

The British Viceroy of India, Lord Wavell, is shown the scene of the Calcutta riots.

2
Religious forces

According to the 1941 census of British India, the total population was 389 million, made up of 255 million Hindus, 92 million Muslims, 6.3 million Christians, 5.6 million Sikhs and 30.1 million others. The religious forces that went on the rampage in Calcutta were released by the snapping of the political tension that had built up during June and July of 1946 between some of these groups. The hatred displayed by Hindus, Muslims and Sikhs stemmed largely from their faiths, which professed tolerance for each other yet were mutually exclusive. The fundamentals of these three faiths therefore demand consideration here.

In a Hindu temple in Delhi, a priest offers prayers before the images of Lord Vishnu and his consort Lakshmi.

Hinduism

Hinduism, the religion of the majority of Indians, has developed over 4,000 years through continuous change and adaptation. It has no founder but it possesses many ancient sacred texts from which have been developed codes of conduct. Generally speaking, a modern Hindu accepts the authority of the Hindu scriptures, the *Vedas*, the *Vedānta Sūtras*, and the *Bhagavadgītā*; believes in *Karma* (the effect of one's actions) and rebirth; worships One God through different images and performs *dharma* (moral duty)

Hindu pilgrims face the rising sun, pray and bathe in the river Ganges. The pot is for carrying away the water.

A priest reads the Hindu scriptures to pilgrims beside the Ganges at the end of the day.

In Calcutta, 200,000 Muslims pray to celebrate the end of the fast month of Ramadan.

according to a clearly-defined system of class, caste, stage of life and family tradition. Unlike many other religions, Hindus do not gather in large groups to worship together. There is much stress on *satya* (truth) and *ahimsa* (non-injury) but these are not always put into practice.

14

Islam

The Muslims in India, as elsewhere, follow the teachings of Muhammad (AD 570–632), the prophet of Islam, who lived in Arabia. Islam, the way of submission to God, developed around the teaching of Muhammad, who was considered to have received the true and full revelation of God. A Muslim is expected to believe in Faith, Action and Spiritual Realization. God – Allah – alone is real. Everything else is His creation and depends on Him. The way to serve God is revealed through Muhammad in the Qur'an, the scripture of Islam. A Muslim must pray five times a day, fast for one month each year, give a part of his earnings to charity and go on a pilgrimage to Mecca, holy city of Islam. These four elements of Action, along with faith, constitute the five pillars of Islam.

Muslims are convinced that there is no other God but Allah and that part of their sacred duty lies in bringing others to this realization. The *mosque* – a place of worship – has no images. Muslims worship together in congregations. Under the brotherhood of Islam everyone is equal, but in the India of 1946, 90 per cent of Muslims were the descendants of converts from the lower castes of Hindu society during seven centuries of Muslim rule, and, therefore, had a caste system of their own. In Muslim as well as Hindu society the upper classes were far removed from the poorer, lower orders in refinement and education. Hinduism and Islam, with diametrically opposite beliefs, had existed side by side without greatly changing each other's beliefs for almost 1,000 years.

Sikhism

Sikhism was founded by Guru Nanak (1469–1539), who was born into a high-ranking Hindu family in the Punjab. He had rejected both Islam and Hinduism but was influenced by the devotional movement of Hinduism and some religious and social values of Islam; for instance, there are no images in a *gurdwara* (a Sikh place of worship) and all are equal in Sikhism. Between 1469 and 1699, there were ten *Gurus* (leaders or teachers) who saw the sect grow into a religion distinct from Islam and Hinduism. The teachings of the first five Gurus, as well as those of some non-Sikhs, were collected into a scripture called the *Ādi-Granth* (Original Collection), which in its present form is known as the *Guru Granth Sāhib* (Collection of Sacred Wisdom), replacing the human Gurus after the tenth leader Guru Gobind Singh (1675–1708). This Guru created the *Khalsa* (pure order) who, as a sign of loyalty to the faith, were enjoined to wear the five 'Ks', namely *Kesh* (hair), *Kangha* (comb), *Kirpan* (sword or dagger), *Kara* (wrist guard) and *Kach* (short pants), which, to this day, are the external symbols of the faithful. After initiation into the Pure Order, the men are called 'singh' and the women 'kaur'. Though Sikhism urges full equality of castes and sexes, social norms of discrimination have often triumphed over noble aims.

Sikhs believe in a formless God which is realized through

A young Sikh prays before entering the inner shrine of the Golden Temple at Amritsar.

human effort, love and meditation. Sikhism is influenced by the Hindu *Bhakti* movement (devotion to a personal God); by the practices of Tantric Yoga; by Sufi devotionalism, and the strict monotheism of Orthodox Islam, thus, in a way, combining the best of many Indian traditions.

These religious forces, enacting a tragedy quite contrary to their respective beliefs, were motivated by the political moves and counter-moves of the British Raj, the Muslim League and the Indian National Congress.

Reading the Guru Granth Sahib – the Sikh scripture – in the Golden Temple of Amritsar.

3
The Three-Nation Contest

The year 1857 was a landmark in both British and Indian history. The British-owned East India Company, founded in 1600, had originally arrived in India for trade. During the following 250 years it had ousted European rivals and gradually increased its power. As British involvement in Indian affairs grew, so did Indian resentment. Lord Dalhousie had annexed a number of Indian kingdoms to

The coat of arms of the British East India Company whose increasing power caused resentment among Indians.

18

the Company's territory, ignoring the Hindu custom of adoption of heirs. This interference in social, religious and political matters by foreign rulers had offended Indians and deprived the princes of their dignity and kingdoms.

Lord Clive is granted the right of Dominion over Bengal, Orissa and Bihar.

Opposite: *The scene of destruction at Lucknow in 1857 – the town was mined by Indians who were rebelling against British rule.*

Below: *British forces attack Indians rebelling against British rule, at Cawnpore in 1857.*

The Raj

In 1857 there was a significant rebellion in North India against British rule. The British termed it 'The Indian Mutiny'; Indians prefer to call it 'The First War of Independence'. It did not result in Indian independence, but it shook both Britain and India. There were atrocities on both sides and, after the rebellion was crushed, the old order changed. The East India Company came to an end and India became part of the British Empire; Queen Victoria took the title Empress of India and the Raj – the British government of India – was founded. The New Order promised not to interfere in social or religious matters, almost 600 Indian princes retained their States, and the destinies of the British nation and India were linked.

Queen Victoria, Empress of India, works on her papers at Frogmore, watched by her Indian attendant.

The spread of Western culture

The foundation of universities at Bombay, Calcutta and Madras in 1857, and later in Punjab and Allahabad, rapidly spread English education and western science. Hindus took full advantage of it, thus preparing themselves to enter the Indian Civil Service after 1871, albeit in subordinate posts. Muslims were conservative in attitude, so they kept away from the new educational opportunites, which were by no means widespread. The introduction of railways, post and telegraph services had improved communications and enabled the Indian Army, with its British officers, to protect the Raj from external and internal dangers. Higher ranks in the Army, the Judiciary and the Civil Service were for the British only, and the political department kept the Indian States under strict control. The Governor-General had autocratic power and ruled with the help of the provincial Governors, the Civil Service and the Army. In his relations with the Indian States as the Crown representative he was styled the Viceroy.

This political and material superiority, coupled with a firm belief in its own racial superiority, took British rule to the zenith of its Imperial greatness at the turn of the nineteenth century.

Towards an independent India

While the Raj functioned for the benefit of Britain, Hindus discovered their past through the efforts made by British scholars to introduce the classical language, Sanskrit, to the West. There were reform movements within Hinduism, such as the Brahmo Samaj, founded by Ram Mohan Roy in 1828, and the Arya Samaj founded by Dayananda in 1875. These movements united Hindus against both Islam and Christianity, and the re-conversion of former Hindus, attempted by the Arya Samaj, alarmed Muslims. Hindus began to think of a Hindu nation, but the foundation of the Indian National Congress in 1885, largely through the efforts of A. O. Hume (1829–1912), a retired British civilian, brought together Indians of different religions to discuss social matters. The aims of the Congress in 1888 were to fuse all Indians into one national whole, to regenerate the nation along intellectual, moral, social and political lines and to consolidate the union of Britain and India by improving conditions in India.

Muslim reaction to a Unified India

There was vehement reaction from Muslims. During the 700 years of Muslim rule, the higher posts in the Civil Service and the Army had been taken up by Muslims. With the advent of British rule, Muslims were replaced by the British in the higher posts and by English-speaking Hindus in subordinate posts in both the Civil Service and the Judiciary. For about twenty years after the Mutiny, Muslims were not favoured by the British, and they had not taken up English education. These two factors held the Muslims back, but this repression came to a halt in the 1870s through the efforts of W. W. Hunter and Syed Ahmad Khan (1817–98). Hunter pointed out to the Government the anti-British feeling among Muslims, and Syed Ahmad Khan founded the Anglo-Oriental College at Aligarh in 1875, which provided Islamic as well as English education. It produced candidates for government service and Muslim political leaders.

In 1887 a middle-class Muslim was elected president of the National Congress. Syed Ahmad Khan wrote to him pointing out that Congress could not be termed 'National' because there were two nations in India, one Hindu, the other Muslim. Because of the British change of policy, Muslims remained loyal to the Government and the Aligarh Movement worked to improve the lot of the Muslims. However, in 1888 nearly a million middle-class Muslims were with the Congress, which was formed to represent all Indians.

Social divisions

Upper-class Hindus and Muslims remained loyal to the Government and opposed Congress. In 1905 Bengal was partitioned for 'administrative reasons' and in 1906 the All-India Muslim League was formed in Dacca to promote and advance the political rights and interests of Muslims. Congress opposed the partition, using Hindu symbols, and this turned the Muslims against Congress. When the Muslims were placed on a separate electorate in 1909, entitled to return only Muslim members to the legislatures, the three-nation contest between the British, the Muslims and the Hindu-dominated Congress really began.

Jinnah and Gandhi

Congress had remained a middle-class affair, not achieving much either through constitutional means or terrorism and boycott. Two of its members, however, went on to play vital roles in modern history. Muhammad Ali Jinnah, who was to become the founder of Pakistan, joined Congress in 1905. At first he was an ardent nationalist. While keeping his Congress Party membership, and in fact becoming its President, he also joined the Muslim League. For a while he managed to keep the peace between both parties, but this was not to last.

Mahatma Gandhi, whose name is known world-wide for his work on behalf of Indian independence, studied law in London and spent twenty-one years in South Africa, from 1893 to 1914, fighting for the rights and dignity of Indians there. He developed his ideas of *Satyāgraha* (insistence upon truth, and peaceful civil disobedience) in South Africa, and he put these ideas into practice after he returned to India and joined the Congress in 1915.

Muhammad Ali Jinnah, leader of the Muslim League, and Mahatma Gandhi, campaigner for Indian independence, together as members of the National Congress.

Disillusionment with Britain

The revocation of the partition of Bengal in 1911 meant the loss of the Muslim majority in that province, which created anti-British feeling among Muslims. Convinced that the British had a sense of justice and fair play, Indians gave £100 million and 50,000 lives to support Britain in World War I. The League and Congress had agreed at Lucknow in 1916 to co-operate for Indian self-rule within the Empire, but when the British Government declared its policy in 1917 and implied that India was not yet ready for self-rule, and when Indian troops under General Dyer fired on 20,000 unarmed Indian civilians at Jallianwala Bagh at Amritsar in 1919, killing 379 and wounding 1,208, both Congress and the League lost faith in British promises and justice.

The Montagu – Chelmsford (Montford) Reforms 1919

This Bill, finally implemented in 1921, represented a major step onwards to self-government, envisaged at first as similar to that of Australia or Canada, within the Empire. Important aspects of the reforms were provincialisation of authority, as well as the introduction of provincial ministerial responsibility; a system of gradual reforms in government and political operation; and the dyarchic principle in provincial government, by which one section of executives (Governor's Executive Council) was responsible solely to the Governor, with the other section to the new elected legislatures. There was also a division of administrative responsibility; the Governor and his Council had charge of 'reserved subjects', concerning administration of justice, the police, irrigation, and development, while ministers responsible to the legislatures were concerned with 'transferred subjects', for example, agriculture, education, public works, health, and other such matters of local concern. Indians now shared this legislative responsibility at senior level, and Indians' suffrage rights were extended to provide an elective body to vote in members of provincial legislatures. Constituencies were of two types: 'general' and 'special', the latter representing special interest groups, for example, universities, and industry. The 'general' constituencies were further split into 'general' and 'reserved', which had far-reaching consequences, since minority groups such as Muslims, Christians, Sikhs, Europeans and Anglo-Indians ('reserved' sections)

The Indian Cavalry in France during the First World War.

enjoyed the allocation of specified numbers of legislative seats in areas where they were substantially represented. Thus communal representation in Indian politics was institutionalized for the first time.

After the scheduled review of the Montford Reforms, the Government of India Act, 1935, introduced the federal principle, provincial autonomy, and a reorganization of provinces, which were the basis of the 1937 and 1945 elections. Political participation in the preparations for the 1935 Act was seen to be Hindu-dominated and Muslims saw their provincial political influence waning. They would control only the Frontier Province and Sind through the principle of majority rule; Bengal they could control only through coalition; in Punjab they just failed to muster a majority. Jinnah, seeing the likely ineffectiveness of the Muslim voice, withdrew from Indian politics to London to practise law.

Bombay in 1930 – Gandhi's secretary addressing a meeting of 100,000 people. They voted to boycott British goods as part of their non-violent opposition to British rule.

Gandhi's non-violent opposition

Gandhi had been successful in his methods of *Satyāgraha* on behalf of farmers in Bihar in 1917 and he decided to use it against the British. His first attempt in 1919 failed, but a year later he decided to try again when he secured control over Congress at the Nagpur session in December 1920. Jinnah opposed Gandhi but was shouted down, causing him to leave Congress after fifteen years of close association.

27

The non-violent, non-co-operation movement, which Gandhi launched, worked well for six months in 1921, but there were riots in Malabar and Bombay. After Congress supporters killed twenty-one policemen at Chauri-chaura village in the United Province, Gandhi suspended the movement in February 1922, thinking that the country as a whole was not ready for non-violent civil disobedience.

Defying the Salt Laws

Communal tension continued to grow between Hindus and Muslims and, in 1927, Muslims were ready to fight in defence of Islam against Hindus. At Lahore session in 1929 Congress declared full independence as its goal. In March 1930, Gandhi started his civil disobedience movement against the 'Salt Laws', laws by which the Government maintained a monopoly over the production and sale of salt. Reaching the west coast after a 322 km (208 mile) march, he broke the law by making salt from seawater on the beach. Gandhi and 60,000 supporters were imprisoned for breaking the salt laws.

The Round Table conference in London, to consider Dominion status for India, achieved little and in 1932 Gandhi re-started the Civil Disobedience Movement. This time the Government arrested prominent Congress leaders and Congress was outlawed. The Movement was officially discontinued in May 1934.

Gandhi's followers defy the Salt Laws: they are extracting the salt from sea water as part of the civil disobedience campaign.

Gandhi's role in the independence movement was unique; his *Satyāgraha* against an Imperial Power was a new concept in politics. By his own example he taught Indians to be fearless and he strove for Hindu-Muslim unity and a united free India to the very last. His dreams were not realized because he under-estimated the desire of Muslims to have their own nation.

Gandhi at the Round Table Conference in London, which discussed Dominion Status for India. No agreement was reached.

A proposed Muslim State

Dr. Muhammad Iqbal, a poet-politician from the Punjab, had for the first time in 1930 conceived the idea of a separate Muslim State comprised of the Muslim provinces of the Punjab, North-West Frontier Province, Sind and Baluchistan. Iqbal and Liaquat Ali Khan, a North Indian politician, persuaded Muhammad Ali Jinnah to return to India from Britain, where he had been practising law since 1932. Jinnah returned and was elected permanent President of the Muslim League in December 1933.

Muhammad Ali Jinnah, campaigner for a separate Muslim State, visits the East London Mosque in 1946.

When the 1935 Government of India Act gave the provinces the right to elect assemblies, Congress secured a majority in seven out of eleven. In the 1937 elections Jinnah urged independent co-operation with Congress in provinces with Hindu majorities, stating: 'We shall always be glad to co-operate with Congress in their constructive programme.' Congress, however, adopted a policy tending rather to absorption, thus increasing Muslim fears of Hindu domination; Jinnah therefore found strong popular support for the idea of a Muslim state: 'The majority community have clearly shown their hand that Hindustan is for the Hindu,' was his conclusion. In 1939, Congress ministers resigned, refusing to support Britain in what was to be World War II. Many Muslims, however, did support Britain, which increased Jinnah's stature in the political arena. Congress started its 'Quit India' movement in 1942, to rid India of British rule, and Jinnah, who had spent many years working to unite Hindus and Muslims, and who was once the President of Congress, began to work actively towards a separate Muslim State.

Below: *A map of pre-Partition India. Compare it with the map of post-Partition India on page 41.*

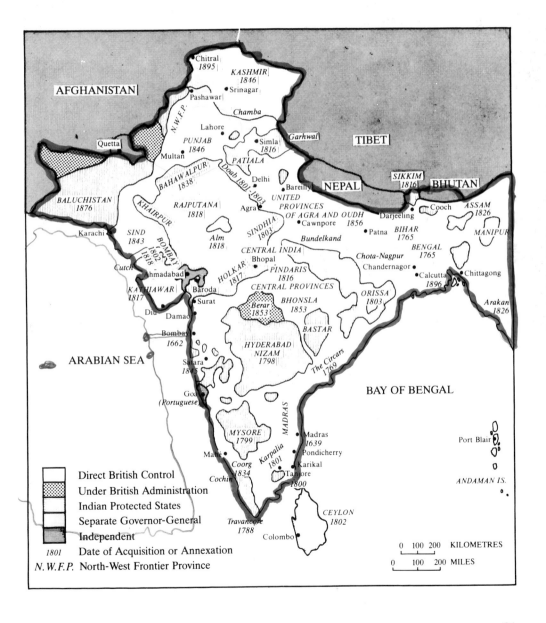

4

'Divide and Quit'

In 1940 Muhammad Ali Jinnah was by no means the undisputed spokesman of all Indian Muslims, although he was the leader of the Muslim League. The League had demanded a separate Muslim state the previous year and obtained an assurance from the Viceroy, Lord Linlithgow, that no decision would be taken over Congress's demand for independence without the approval and consent of the League. After the failure of the Cripps Mission in March 1942, Congress launched its 'Quit India' movement in August and was promptly outlawed; thousands were back in jail.

The Muslim League grows in power
The situation changed rapidly in favour of Jinnah; between September 1942 and May 1943 Muslim League ministries were formed in Sind, Bengal and the North-West Frontier Province. The position in the Punjab also changed when the unionist party leader, Sir Sikandar Hayat Khan, died in December 1942; the League's influence there began to increase. Jinnah could now claim to speak for all Muslims in India, and when Linlithgow left as Viceroy in October 1943, Jinnah asked the League to adopt the slogan: 'Divide and Quit'.

Gandhi was released from prison in May 1944 and wanted to meet Jinnah. The meeting was arranged in September, but nothing came of it. Muslims throughout India thought, however, that Gandhi had accepted Jinnah as the spokesman for all Muslims and, in consequence, Jinnah's popularity with the Muslim masses greatly increased.

Failure of the Simla Conference
The new Viceroy, Lord Wavell, held a political conference at Simla in June 1945 to discuss the nomination of equal numbers of Hindus and Muslims to the Viceroy's council, which was to form a transitional government. Jinnah

Clement Attlee, leader of the British Labour Government, which favoured the transfer of power to Indians, and called a general election in India in December 1945.

insisted that all Muslim nominations must be made by the League only and that Congress could not nominate any Muslims in its quota. Since Congress had always represented all Indians it rejected Jinnah's claim. Although the League did not have the support of all Muslims in the Punjab and Bengal, Jinnah insisted that the League should be accepted as the sole representative body for Indian Muslims. The conference failed.

A general election
The British Labour Government, under Clement Attlee, was determined to transfer power in India to Indians, and so decided to assess the strength of Congress and the League by holding a general election in India in December 1945.

In the Central Assembly, Congress gained a clear majority and it formed ministries in the six Hindu-majority provinces. The Muslim League won a majority of seats only in Bengal and, although Congress and the League had won an equal number of seats in Sind – a Muslim majority province – the League was allowed to form a ministry there. In Assam, Punjab and the North-West Frontier Province, Congress retained control; the Unionist ministry in the Punjab needed Congress support for survival, but the League was the largest party, although without an overall majority. The revolt of ratings in the Royal Indian Navy at Bombay and Karachi in February 1946 convinced the British Government that they could no longer hold India by force of arms.

Moving towards a free India

Prime Minister Attlee announced in February 1946 that a special Cabinet Mission, consisting of Lord Pethick-Lawrence, Secretary of State for India, Sir Stafford Cripps, President of the Board of Trade, and A. V. Alexander, First Lord of the Admiralty, would be sent to India to work out a constitution for a free India. The mission arrived in Delhi in March 1946 and met leaders of all parties and communities. The main discussions, however, were with Azad, the Muslim President of Congress, and Jinnah, the leader of the Muslim League. Jinnah demanded a Pakistan comprising the six Muslim provinces, but as East Punjab, West Bengal and Assam had Hindu districts, the demand was rejected.

Muhammad Ali Jinnah, leader of the Muslim League, and Sir Stafford Cripps, British President of the Board of Trade, discuss negotiations for the self-government of India at New Delhi in 1946.

Jawaharlal Nehru, elected President of Congress in July 1946.

The Cabinet Mission plan

The Cabinet Mission plan rejected the division of the country into two separate sovereign states, but envisaged transfer of power to a union of India which would deal with foreign affairs, defence and communications from a central government. Hindu and Muslim provinces were to be grouped into three sections, A, B and C, keeping Muslim provinces together in sections B and C. This dispelled Muslim fears of being engulfed in Hindu culture. The three groups were to be autonomous except in foreign affairs, defence and communications, and the provinces could not secede from the union.

Rejection of the Cabinet Mission plan

This long-term plan was at first accepted by both Congress and the League. On 7 July 1946, Nehru was elected Congress President and in his speech he implied that as soon as Congress went into Constituent Assembly it was free to do anything. Then, on 10 July, Nehru gave a press conference in which he apparently contradicted the Mission's plan. Jinnah construed this as the complete repudiation of the plan by Congress. He promptly asked the council of the League to reject the Cabinet Mission plan, which it did, unanimously, on 29 July. Jinnah then fixed 16 August 1946 as Direct Action Day. In a fiery speech on 28 July, Jinnah vehemently declared his opposition to the British Government and Congress. His goal was an independent Pakistan. His war cry was 'Quit, but Divide and Quit!'

5

Towards a 'moth-eaten' Pakistan

After the shock of the Calcutta killings on Direct Action Day, Congress formed an interim government and Wavell persuaded Jinnah to join it. Jinnah did not join personally but nominated five Leaguers, including Liaquat Ali Khan, to join it and wreck it from within, which the League members effectively did. On 20 February 1947, Attlee announced in Parliament that the British Government intended to withdraw from India not later than June 1948; that the British Government would transfer power to some form of central government for British India and to some provincial governments, in the absence of an agreed constitution; and that Lord Mountbatten would be the new Viceroy. No reason for Lord Wavell's replacement was offered, though from his journal it would appear that differences of opinion over official policy, particularly with reference to Congress, had arisen.

Lord Mountbatten, the new Viceroy, is greeted by Jawaharlal Nehru, leader of India's interim Government, in March 1947.

Mountbatten as Viceroy

The League intensified communal rioting in the Punjab; the Chief Minister of the Muslim-Hindu-Sikh coalition resigned. On 8 March, the Congress working committee demanded partition of Punjab and Bengal to protect Hindus. Lord Mountbatten reached Delhi on 22 March. He had only fifteen months to bring British rule in India to an end. To achieve success in this near-impossible task he put forward three conditions: that he must have full power to take decisions without interference from London; that he could choose his personal staff; and that he could re-join the Royal Navy when his work was done, without loss of seniority. Attlee agreed without any reservations.

Mountbatten met the Indian leaders individually while Lady Mountbatten and their daughter worked on social diplomacy through daughters and sisters of some of the Indian leaders. V. P. Menon, an astute Hindu civil servant, who was Reforms Commissioner and constitutional adviser

Lord and Lady Mountbatten – they were to be the last Viceroy and Vicereine of India.

to Linlithgow, Wavell and Mountbatten, persuaded Val-labh-bhai Patel, a prominent Congressman and later Deputy Prime Minister, that division of the country was better than civil war, while on 20 April Nehru declared in a public speech that the Muslim League could have Pakistan minus the Hindu areas of Assam, West Bengal and East Punjab.

Vallabh-bhai Patel, Deputy Prime Minister of India, was eventually persuaded that division of the country was necessary in order to avoid civil war.

Lord Mountbatten and Muhammad Ali Jinnah meet at New Delhi to discuss the transfer of power.

The transfer of power begins

Mountbatten evolved a plan to transfer power to the existing Constituent Assembly, while giving an option to the Muslim provinces either to join the Indian union or to form independent states. Other groups such as the Princely States, the Sikhs, the Pathans, and the Nagas began to demand their own separate states. The Viceroy decided to transfer power on 15 August 1947.

V. P. Menon suggested the transfer of power to two Dominions of India and Pakistan within the Commonwealth. The Mountbatten plan was amended, the independent option was dropped, and Nehru accepted it on 11 May. Baldev Singh, the Sikh representative, also accepted it, but Jinnah refused to commit himself in writing. He was afraid that the Muslim community would not accept a truncated Pakistan. In addition, the aging Jinnah was suffering from a terminal illness; it was unlikely he would ever be head of state in Pakistan because under the revised plan there was to be only one Governor-General for both Dominions.

Agreement about partition

After consulting Attlee in London, the Viceroy returned to Delhi and presented the plan to the Indian leaders on 2 June. Congress and the Sikhs accepted it openly, but Jinnah simply nodded his assent. Attlee announced the plan in the Commons on the following day. The people of the Muslim provinces were to choose whether they wanted to join India or Pakistan. The Princely States were free either to remain independent or to join India or Pakistan.

At last there was all-party agreement, and for Congress

an end to its sixty-two-year struggle for independence from the British Raj. The civil service, the armed forces, the cash and the equipment needed for the huge administration were all to be partitioned; the boundaries of the new States would have to be demarcated. As expected, Muslim East Bengal, West Punjab, Sylhet, Sind, Baluchistan and the North-West Frontier Province opted for Pakistan. The Hindu and Sikh districts in East Punjab and Hindu areas of West Bengal, including Calcutta, chose India.

A map of post-Partition India.

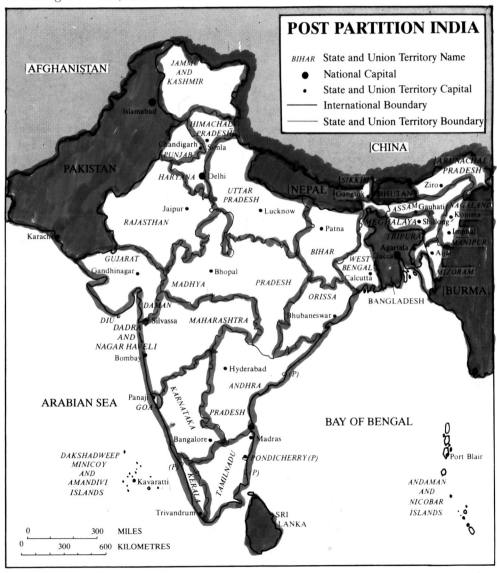

41

The Indian Independence Bill

On 4 July the Indian Independence Bill, designed to transfer power to the new Dominions of India and Pakistan on 15 August 1947, was introduced in the House of Commons, and it received the Royal Assent on 18 July.

The armed forces were divided on a territorial basis by the Joint Defence Council under Field Marshal Sir Claude Auchinleck. Sir Cyril Radcliffe was appointed chairman of the two boundary commissions to demarcate the boundaries of East and West Bengal and of East and West Punjab.

Drawing the boundaries

Each Boundary Commission, in accordance with the plan of 3 June 1947, consisted of a chairman and four members, all High Court Judges, two nominated by the Congress and two by the Muslim League. The awards of the boundary commissions were not made public until 17 August, two days after independence.

On 2 July, Jinnah told the Viceroy that he himself wanted to be Governor-General of Pakistan, but Congress invited Mountbatten to become Governor-General of Free India, which he accepted.

There was still the big question of the future of the Princely States, which occupied two-fifths of the land of the sub-continent and ruled over 100 million people. If India were not to be split into small independencies these 570 states had to be persuaded to join either India or Pakistan before 15 August.

Members of the Anti-Pakistan Front carrying black flags and fasting, in protest against the division of the country into the two independent Dominions of India and Pakistan.

The Indian Union

Nehru's interim government had created a States Department. V. P. Menon, as its secretary, prepared a plan which offered the States independent status within the union in all matters except foreign affairs, defence and communications. When the plan was approved by Patel, Menon requested Mountbatten to sponsor the Instrument of Accession. On 25 July, Lord Mountbatten, dressed in full uniform, addressed major ruling princes and state representatives, asking them to join the Indian Union before 15 August, after which date he would not be able to help them. Most

Voting on the partition issue at the Legislative Assembly in Calcutta, June 1947, in preparation for Independence. Hindu West Bengal elected to join India, whilst Muslim East Bengal chose Pakistan.

43

In 1947, violence broke out between Hindus and Muslims over partition. These Hindu shops in Lahore have been destroyed by rioters.

agreed to join India. By the date of independence, only Hyderabad, Kashmir and Junagadh had not acceded to either union. In these three cases the Indian army became involved; it occupied Kashmir almost immediately, Junagadh in October 1947, and Hyderabad on 17 September 1948. No Hindu state joined Pakistan.

During the communal riots in the Punjab before 15 August, Lady Mountbatten bravely visited the affected areas and helped to relieve the sufferings of the people by taking much-needed medical assistance.

When Jinnah went to Karachi a few days before 15 August, he left behind more Muslims ready to live in India than there were in West Pakistan. Jinnah preferred to accept – after all the strife, political gamesmanship, and much bloodshed – what came to be known as a 'moth-eaten' Pakistan rather than no Pakistan at all.

Muhammad Ali Jinnah, who had long dreamt of a separate Muslim state, became leader of the independent Dominion of Pakistan on 14 August 1947.

6

The transfer of power

Opposite: *Jinnah, now Governor-General, with Lord and Lady Mountbatten at the ceremony at Karachi marking the transfer of power from Britain to the Dominion of Pakistan, 14 August 1947.*

The British Raj was about to come to an end. The last Viceroy, Lord Mountbatten, flew to Karachi on 13 August and inaugurated the independent Muslim Dominion of Pakistan the next day. Although the Cabinet was headed by Liaquat Ali Khan, that very day Jinnah assumed for himself supreme power in all fields of Government. He became Pakistan personified; his dream, for which he had worked tirelessly, was finally realized: a Muslim State carved out of the Raj. His political triumph was complete.

Below: *The formal ceremony in Karachi, 18 August 1947. Jinnah as Governor-General witnesses Liaquat Ali Khan's installation as Prime Minister of the new state of Pakistan.*

The Transfer of Power

In Delhi, 15 August 1947, Jawaharlal Nehru is sworn in as the first Prime Minister of Free India by Lord Mountbatten. Rajendra Prasad, Vallabh-bhai Patel, Maulana Azad and Baldev Singh become members of the new cabinet.

Lord and Lady Mountbatten then flew back to Delhi. The Transfer of Power ceremony was to take place at midnight; the members of the Legislative Assembly, wearing their best clothes and white Gandhi caps, assembled to welcome the new Dominion. Nehru, Patel, Azad, Baldev Singh, Raj Gopalachari, Rajendra Prasad, Rajkumari Amrit Kaur and many other leading Congress members were overcome with emotion.

The ceremony in Delhi had even more meaning for the Mountbattens and the British. They had conquered India, made Delhi the capital of the Indian Empire since 1912, and it was at Delhi that the last British Viceroy was to transfer sovereignty to the Indian Constituent Assembly on 14 August 1947, at midnight.

Nehru's 'Tryst with Destiny' speech

As midnight approached, Jawaharlal Nehru made his famous 'Tryst with Destiny' speech, which was broadcast by All-India Radio. This is a short extract:

'Long years ago we made a tryst with destiny, and now the time comes when we shall redeem our pledge, not wholly or in full measure, but very substantially. At the stroke of the midnight hour, when the world sleeps, India will awake to life and freedom. A moment comes, which comes but rarely in history, when we step out from the old to the new, when an age ends, and when the soul of a nation, long suppressed, finds utterance. It is fitting that at this solemn moment we take the pledge of dedication to the service of India and her people and to the still larger cause of humanity.'

At the Midnight Session of the Indian Constituent Assembly, on 14 August 1947, Prime Minister Nehru makes his famous 'Tryst with Destiny' speech, in which he pledges dedication to a new India awakening to life and freedom after years of suppression.

Prime Minister Nehru displays the new National flag of India, on July 23 1947.

Independence Day

The Independence Day celebrations started all over India after midnight. Nehru and Rajendra Prasad went to Vice-regal Lodge in Delhi to make the formal offer of Governor-Generalship to Mountbatten. The first Governor-General of Free India then drove in state to the Assembly House and administered the oath of office to Nehru and his cabinet.

The British Raj, after almost a century of rule, during which it had gradually conquered and unified the country, brought it justice and good government and also exploited its wealth, plundered its riches and patronized its people, was no more.

Violence in the Punjab and Bengal

Mahatma Gandhi was not in Delhi to celebrate, because the partition of India had devastated his dream; he was in Calcutta, trying to prevent Hindus and Muslims from killing each other. He did achieve the impossible, acting as a one-man boundary force in Calcutta and Noakhali, where killings stopped; but the Punjab was another story. The 50,000 strong boundary force there could not prevent Sikhs and Hindus being butchered in Lahore and Muslim women and girls being raped in Amritsar.

People celebrated in many cities and towns, but to the Hindus, Muslims and Sikhs in the Punjab and Bengal, Independence and partition brought nothing but torture, tears and tragedy.

Prime Minister Nehru surveys the Independence Day celebrations at Delhi on the 15 August 1947.

7
The immediate aftermath

As the Independence Day celebrations got under way, statesmen and commentators around the world welcomed the new Dominions and praised the wisdom of Britain in granting India its independence. The anti-British feeling in India, which had gradually grown during the sixty-two-year struggle of Congress for independence, seemed to vanish overnight and there began genuine friendship between the two peoples. The majority of British people, after their long struggle against tyranny in Europe, seemed to appreciate the Indian demand for freedom; except for a few diehard imperialists, the British were glad to be free of their Indian responsibility. Churchill and many Conservatives resented the liquidation of the Indian Empire by the Socialists.

Anti-British feeling turns to friendship. Here at New Delhi, jubilant crowds celebrating the establishment of the new Dominion of India have broken through a police cordon to greet Lord and Lady Mountbatten.

However, the timely transfer of power without any strings attached has ensured friendly relations between India and Britain to the present day, even though relations in 1986 became strained owing to differing approaches to the South African apartheid question and the aid sent by British-based Sikh groups to extremists seeking an independent Sikh state in Punjab.

Boundary disputes

The new goverment experienced its first strain when refugees poured in from West Punjab and East Bengal; a strain which threatened its very existence.

Sir Cyril Radcliffe was appointed Chairman of both boundary commissions; the public sittings of the Bengal Commission took place at Calcutta in July, and again to discuss the question of Sylhet in August. The Punjab Commission met at Lahore in late July 1947. Since there was no agreement between members on important issues in all three places, the Chairman had to make the final award based on information gathered at public sittings and later discussions.

The demands of various parties, such as Congress, the Muslim League, Hindu Mahasabha, Assam Provincial Congress Committee and the Sikh members of the Punjab Legislative Assembly, were too divergent and could not be fully met.

Bengal

The Congress claimed 59 per cent of the area of West Bengal and 46 per cent of its population. Under the Award it received only 36 per cent of the area and 35 per cent of the population, including Calcutta. The rest went to East Pakistan. Only a part of the district of Sylhet, being a Muslim majority area, was to be awarded to East Pakistan, and, as the boundary cut across the railway line, the important junction for Sylhet lay in Assam (India) and not Pakistan.

The Punjab

In the Punjab the matter was complicated because important cities, canal networks and rich farming complexes in the canal colonies were affected by the boundary line between West Punjab (Pakistan) and East Punjab (India). East Punjab received 38 per cent of the area and 45 per cent of the population and gained control over the river systems of Bias, Sutlej and Ravi and the Mandi hydro-

Opposite: *Disputes over the exchange of population between the two new dominions led to Hindu-Muslim rioting. Here Prime Minister Nehru calls for peace at a mass meeting in Delhi, October 1947.*

electric scheme. The Sikhs resented the loss of Lahore and the canal colonies with rich farming lands. The commissions had to achieve this impossible task in about six weeks and inevitably the final award disappointed all interested parties.

The social consequences of partition

The social outcome of the new boundaries was tragically disruptive in many cases; village communities, united for centuries, found themselves split on religious grounds and living in different countries. Punjabi families, whether Hindu, Muslim or Sikh, were split between India and Pakistan. Nationality now reinforced religion in causing violent division, and bloodshed followed closely after political manipulation of territory.

The refugee problem

After the fighting in the Punjab, long columns of refugees began their march to reach their new countries. It is estimated that about half a million died in the Punjab and

Following the partition of India into separate Hindu and Muslim states, millions of refugees had to march for miles to reach their new countries. This is a refugee camp in Calcutta.

Bengal; in addition, five and a half million travelled each way across the frontier in the Punjab. Large numbers of Hindus moved from Sind into India and over a million came from East Pakistan into West Bengal. This migration caused untold misery; Delhi was choked with Muslim refugees and communal violence was expected to erupt against them. Gandhi came to Delhi from Calcutta in October 1947 and successfully completed his mission of reconciliation.

Hindu and Sikh refugees arrive in Bombay, having fled Pakistan in the British-Indian liner Dwarka.

Gandhi defends Muslim claims

The division of assets had started on the 15 August, and there was disagreement in the Cabinet over the payment of large funds to Pakistan, because of the Kashmir dispute. Gandhi started a fast in order to persuade the Indian Government to effect payment to Pakistan; he also wanted safe conduct for Muslim refugees from the capital, Delhi. On both counts the Government acted according to Gandhi's wishes, and he gave up his fast on 18 January 1948.

The assassination of Gandhi

This change of policy by the Government under Gandhi's influence angered the right-wing Hindus; one man, an articulate and educated Hindu, acting as an individual and not a member of any conspiracy, shot Gandhi on the 31 January 1948, as he was proceeding to his daily prayer meeting. The man was later hanged in Ambala jail. The right-wing Hindu organizations were discredited and their political influence gradually diminished. Patel, as Home Minister, was blamed for not protecting the Mahatma effectively.

The removal of Gandhi at the hands of an extremist paradoxically strengthened Nehru's hand in subsequent years. A brief war flared up between India and Pakistan over the question of Kashmir, but it was settled by a United Nations Truce in 1948. The relations between the two countries have remained coldly hostile over the Kashmir issue.

India's new Constitution

A new Constitution was drafted which gave India a federal structure with a strong central government controlling foreign affairs, defence, railways, postal services, ports and currency. The Government of India Act of 1935 was an obvious model for this. The President is the Head of State with reserve powers and there are two Houses of Indian Legislature, the Lok Sabha and Rajya Sabha. The universal franchise and the present population of 750 million (1986) make India the largest democracy in the world.

The body of Mahatma Gandhi lying in state in New Delhi. Gandhi was shot dead on January 31 1948 by a right-wing Hindu, angered by his campaign to protect Muslim refugees.

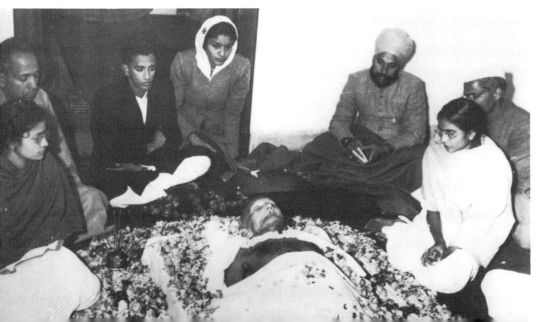

Pakistan after independence

With the partition of India in 1947, Pakistan became a separate republic, with Muhammad Ali Jinnah as Governor-General and Head of State, and Liaquat Ali Khan as Prime Minister. Jinnah had been the founder of Pakistan, and an important unifying force. When he died the following year, 1948, his death was a great loss to the country.

Like India, the new state of Pakistan faced many problems of poverty, economic instability and growing population. But Pakistan had other problems, for it was divided into two parts – West and East Pakistan – separated by northern India. Nor were the people of the two separate areas united in spirit, for they were of different racial and linguistic backgrounds. The language barrier (Urdu being spoken in the West, Bengali in the East) proved an obstacle to promoting national unity. These two widely-separated peoples had to depend on communication with each other by air or sea.

There were trade problems, too, especially for East Pakistan, which produced jute on a vast scale but had no mills to process it and had lost its main export outlet, Calcutta, to India. Armed confrontation with India over Kashmir, and the dispute over the River Indus waters, which India wished to divert for its own use, did not help to promote stability during the first two years of Pakistan's independence.

The Pakistan border. A team of Indian observers for the United Nations is checked through the frontier-post to settle a dispute between villagers on either side.

57

8
The legacy: India

There were three immediate problems for Nehru's government to solve. The Maharaja of Kashmir acceded to India, but Pathan tribesmen from Pakistan had entered Kashmir to occupy a large area. The Indian army was sent in and had to fight relentlessly to win territory. Later, there were political disputes with Sheikh Abdullah, leader of the All Jammu and Kashmir National Conference, before the present state of Jammu and Kashmir saw peace. There was also a dispute with Pakistan over the diversion of irrigation water from the Indus river, but it was resolved in 1960 with the help of the World Bank. Junagadh and Hyderabad were annexed to the Indian Union by force, although their rulers did not wish it. Within two years of independence, with Patel dead and Gandhi murdered, Nehru became the indisputable leader of Government, Congress and the Indian Union. The Union Government now began a new chapter of Indian history.

Opposite: *Famine in Bihar, north of Calcutta. These women have come to tell the district inspector of their plight.*

In September 1947 war broke out between India and Pakistan over Kashmir. These Muslim refugees have fled from Indian-held territory.

Independence for the colonies

Britain's example in releasing India to independence was followed by Holland in Indonesia and France in Indo-China, so within a few years most of South-East Asia became free. African countries in the British Empire began to follow India's lead, and agitated for self-rule within the Commonwealth. Only South Africa and Pakistan have left the Commonwealth; the other former colonies are all members.

Nehru's influence on India

Great problems were inherited from the British Raj, which Nehru, with his vibrant energy and almost autocratic control of Government and Congress, decided to tackle. Large investment in the public sector enabled India to set up three steel plants with British, German and Russian advisers and technical expertise. Gradually, national and personal income increased. Social democratic ideals were never lost sight of and the establishment of universities and technical colleges improved educational opportunities at the top end of the spectrum. Primary and secondary education was expanded later so that literacy, which was about 10 per cent in 1940, reached 36.2 per cent by 1985.

The modernization of Indian industry. Tata Electric Company employs 7,000 technicians at its atomic power station at Trombay.

Rebuilding India

Large-scale irrigation and power projects, such as those at Damodar Valley and Hirakud, coupled with modern techniques and chemical fertilizers, increased food production so that India began to be self-sufficient. Large-scale industrialization increased the national income by 42 per cent during 1951–61. Important legislation affecting Hindu marriage, such as succession rights, and divorce and maintenance, removed a great deal of social injustice.

India's foreign policy, which Nehru controlled for seventeen years, kept her out of power blocs. This neutrality enabled her to deal with domestic problems. Increases in

The control room of the huge Tata Thermal Plant.

Traditional methods being used to irrigate a paddy field in Bengal in eastern India.

personal income and food production are still swallowed up by the vast increase in population, which grew from 434 million in 1961 to 750 million in 1986. Birth control is official government policy, but it seems a losing battle. The greatest strain placed on the Union Government stems from separatism of various regional groups trying to seek political identity through religion or language.

Reorganization of the Indian states

In 1956 there was radical reorganization of the states on a linguistic basis after riots in Andhra; this was followed by the creation of Maharashtra and Gujarat in 1960. The Punjab was divided on a linguistic basis into Punjab and Haryana, with Punjabi the official language in Punjab and Hindi in Haryana. Although Sikhs are slightly in the majority in Punjab, it is not a Sikh state owing to the substantial Hindu minority.

In December 1961 the Indian army invaded the Portuguese colony of Goa, and annexed it to the Indian Union, thus finally ridding India of its colonial past and uniting the country in independence.

The Sikhs demand independence

The present demand for Khalistan, an independent Sikh state, has led to constant terrorist activities. A Sikh government was elected in the Punjab after the assassination of the Prime Minister, Mrs Indira Gandhi (Nehru's daughter) in October 1984. An accord was reached with the moderate Sikh party by her son Rajiv Gandhi, the current Prime Minister. Extremist activities in the Punjab have not abated, however.

The language problem

There has been a long dispute over making Hindi the official language of India. Nehru retained English as the second official language in order to keep the south, where English is widely known but Hindi is not, within the Union. In 1965 Tamil-speakers in Southern India rioted against the use of Hindi. As a result English remains an official language.

India has to spend a large proportion of its national income on defence to secure its borders against threats from its neighbours, Pakistan and China. This unfortunately affects the lives of the Indian people because money is short for education and medical services.

The biggest headache for the government, however, is caused by religious or linguistic questions, which sometimes threaten the secular democracy, a democracy which is so vital for world peace.

The cremation of Mrs Indira Gandhi, Prime Minister of India until her assassination in 1984 by Sikhs demanding an independent Sikh State. Her son Rajiv Gandhi, who followed her as Prime Minister, looks on.

9
The legacy: Pakistan

Under the constitution of Pakistan, as a federal republic within the Commonwealth, Muhammad Ali Jinnah was no mere figurehead. As Governor-General and President of the Constituent Assembly, he controlled the Prime Minister, his cabinet, the assembly and the armed forces, yet he lacked skilled administrators and was forced to recruit British officials to run the machinery of government. There was also deep division between the two halves of the republic. East Pakistan contained just over half the population of the new nation. Its people spoke Bengali and, although Muslim by religion, were culturally different from the Urdu-speaking population of West Pakistan. Karachi, the federal capital, was over 1600 km (1000 miles) from Dacca, the provincial capital of East Pakistan.

Mohammad Ali Jinnah, the founder of Pakistan, died in September 1948. After his death his powers were dispersed among a number of lesser politicians. Liaquat Ali Khan, the new Prime Minister, appeared at first to control the government, the Muslim League and the Constituent Assembly, but he failed to solve the problems of Kashmir, the dispute over the Indus river water (which was vital to Pakistan's irrigation system), the state of the economy, and the refugees. In 1950, Pakistan was still without a Constitution.

In October 1951 Liaquat Ali Khan was assassinated and Khwajia Nazimuddin became Pakistan's second Prime Minister.

Nazimuddin also failed to solve the problems he had inherited. In addition, there arose three new ones: a food crisis due to crop failure, budgetary difficulties due to a fall in the price of jute and cotton, and religious opposition over the Constitutional issue.

In April 1953, Ghulam Mohammad, the Governor-General, dismissed Nazimuddin and his cabinet and chose Mohammad Ali as the next Prime Minister, demonstrating

Opposite: *Liaquat Ali Khan, the first Prime Minister of Pakistan, was assassinated in 1951.*

65

Zulfikar Ali Bhutto, head of the Pakistan People's Party and the country's first democratically elected Prime Minister.

that the Governor-General could control the Prime Minister. Mohammad Ali was a Bengali and East Bengal had 44 out of 74 seats in the Constituent Assembly. The Muslim League was defeated in the 1954 provincial elections in East Bengal by a coalition called the United Front. Mohammad Ali dismissed the United Front provincial government and appointed Major-General Iskandar Mirza as Governor of East Bengal with full powers, thus controlling East Bengal. Iskandar Mirza became Governor-General and President in September 1955.

In the meantime, Ghulam Mohammad, the Governor-General, dissolved the Constituent Assembly and the cabinet. He formed a new cabinet with Mohammad Ali as Prime Minister, three other ministers from the former cabinet and nine new members, who had no seat in the

*General Ayub Khan,
Commander-in-Chief of
the army, who took over
Pakistan in 1958 and
remained President until
1969.*

Assembly – among them General Ayub Khan. After seven
years, Pakistan still had no Constitution and no Constituent
Assembly. Many political parties emerged as the Muslim
League declined in influence; only the Pakistan People's
Party of Zulfikar Ali Bhutto and the Awami League of East
Pakistan brought about significant changes in the life of the
country.

The second Constituent Assembly was elected in June
1955 and a Constitution for the Islamic Republic of Pakistan
was approved in March 1956. Since then there have been
three Constitutions, in 1962, 1969 and 1973, each replacing
the previous one.

A Pakistani tank passes a cart carrying local civilians in the battle-zone of the India-Pakistan war, September 1965.

In 1958, General Ayub Khan, the Commander-in-chief of the armed forces, took over Pakistan, suspended the Constitution, abolished political parties and tried to run the country with the help of the army. A new capital was built at Islamabad, and in 1960 a system of 'basic democracy' (later included in the 1962 Constitution), was introduced, under which Ayub Khan was appointed President for five years, with the cabinet making all the decisions instead of the Legislature. Ayub Khan was forced to resign during his second term in 1969, when Yahya Khan took over as President.

There were elections during which the Awami League, led by Sheikh Mujibur Rahman, won in East Bengal; Ali Bhutto's Pakistan People's Party won in West Pakistan. The Awami League wished to break away from control by West Pakistan. The army tried to control East Bengal but failed, and, with India's intervention in 1971, East Pakistan broke away to become a separate country, called Bangladesh.

When Yahya Khan resigned, Zulfikar Ali Bhutto became Pakistan's first democratically elected Prime Minister. In 1972 he took the country out of the Commonwealth. He appeared to provide a stable, democratic administration, but to many his rule was authoritarian and high-handed. In the 1977 elections his party won, but the opposition accused him of ballot rigging. Riots followed; he was forced to call in the army to restore order. In July 1977, Bhutto was overthrown by General Zia ul-Haq, who suspended the Constitution. Bhutto was found guilty of conspiracy to murder in 1978 and hanged in April 1979. General Zia has been in power since 1977, becoming President in 1978.

General Zia, who deposed Prime Minister Bhutto in 1977 and suspended the Constitution, to become President in 1978.

Since 1971, Pakistan has consisted of only the Western sector, where Islamic law is enforced. The strain of wars with India in 1965 and against East Pakistan in 1971, together with political instability and social unrest, have

Sheikh Mujib, Prime Minister of Bangladesh, which separated from West Pakistan in 1971, arrives in Pakistan for a reconciliation with Prime Minister Bhutto. Mujib was assassinated in 1975.

slowed down economic development. Much needs to be done about land reform, education and social services, but these areas progress rapidly when under a system of government which appears to have the people's support.

Foreign policy is dominated by Pakistan's membership of SEATO, the Baghdad Pact (CENTO), and her fear of the aggression of India, which makes the country heavily reliant on American aid for both money and armaments, as well as remittances from migrant labour overseas.

Bangladesh has faced huge problems since 1971: food shortages, poverty, flooding and racial tension. In 1975, Sheikh Mujib and his family were assassinated, as were several of his successors.

In recent years both Pakistan and Bangladesh have taken part in the development of a new, stricter form of Islam and have received economic help from Arab oil-producing countries. There are still many problems to face in India, Pakistan and Bangladesh, however. Gandhi's dream of a united Indian sub-continent seems more remote than ever.

Poverty in Bangladesh. A destitute woman in Bhairave lives on a footpath surrounded by her possessions.

Date Chart

1857–1859	The Indian Mutiny (The First War of Independence). The British Crown begins to rule India. Lord Canning becomes first Viceroy.
1885	The Indian National Congress founded.
1898–1905	Lord Curzon Viceroy of India.
1906	Foundation of the All India Muslim League.
1909	Muslims placed on a separate electorate.
1911	Announcement that Delhi will be the future Imperial capital.
1915	Gandhi returns to India from South Africa. Congress and the Muslim League form an alliance.
1917	Gandhi starts his first *Satyāgraha* in Bihar.
1919	Amritsar massacre.
1920	Mohammad Ali Jinnah leaves Congress.
1921	Central Legislature inaugurated.
1929	Nehru elected President of Congress and demands complete independence for India.
1930	Gandhi starts the Civil Disobedience movement against the Salt Tax. Congress is outlawed; its leaders arrested.
1930–32	Three Round Table Conferences in London.
1932	Congress leaders arrested.
1935	Government of India Act passed.
1942	Cripps Mission to India. 'Quit India' Movement by Congress. Congress outlawed, its leaders arrested.
1945	Simla Conference fails.
1946	June – Cabinet Mission plan accepted by Congress and the Muslim League. July – The League rejects the Mission plan. August – Direct Action Day – Calcutta killings. October – The League joins the Interim Government.
1947	February – British intention of leaving India made public. March – Lord Mounbatten replaces Wavell as Viceroy.

	May – Menon-Mountbatten plan accepted by Nehru.
	2 June – The plan for the partition of India accepted by Congress, Sikhs and the League.
	15 August – India and Pakistan become independent. Nehru and Liaquat Ali Khan head the respective Cabinets.
1948	Mahatma Gandhi shot dead in Delhi. Mohammad Ali Jinnah dies.
1950	India becomes a Republic within the British Commonwealth.
1951	Liaquat Ali Khan assassinated.
1956	New constitution declares Pakistan an Islamic Republic.
1958	Ayub Khan becomes President of Pakistan.
1962	'Basic democracy' included in Pakistan's new Constitution.
1964	Death of Nehru.
1965	In India, Tamil riots against Hindi language. English continues as an official language.
1966	Mrs Indira Gandhi, Nehru's daughter, becomes Indian Prime Minister.
1969	Pakistan's Constitution revised; Yahya Khan becomes President.
1971	East Pakistan secedes and becomes Bangladesh, with Sheikh Mujibur Rahman as Prime Minister.
1972	Zulfikar Ali Bhutto elected Prime Minister of Pakistan.
1975	Mujibur Rahman assassinated.
1977	Zulfikar Ali Bhutto elected as Pakistan's Prime Minister, and later overthrown. Constitution suspended.
1978	Gen. Zia ul-Haq becomes President of Pakistan.
1979	Zulfikar Ali Bhutto hanged for conspiracy to murder.
1983	Gen. Ershad assumes Presidency of Bangladesh.
1984	Sikh extremists force Indian army to attack Golden Temple at Amritsar.
	Indira Gandhi assassinated.
	Rajiv Gandhi, her son, becomes Prime Minister of India.

Glossary

Baghdad Pact Treaty for mutual defence signed by Turkey, Pakistan, Iraq and Iran. Renamed CENTO in 1959.

British East India Company The company founded in 1600 to engage in trade with the East.

Cabinet Mission A group of officials sent by Clement Attlee to India to work out a new constitution for a free India.

Caste A Hindu system that divides Indian people into many different occupational groups.

Civil disobedience *Satyāgraha*, Gandhi's method of non-violent non-co-operation with the British in India during the struggle for independence.

Congress, Indian National Political group founded in 1885 to promote Indians' interests by constitutional means.

Dominion A completely self-governing colony, associated with the mother-country but not subordinate to it.

Goonda A hired thug, prepared to use force and even to kill.

Hartal A non-violent boycott used as a political weapon by disrupting commerce, transport and administration.

Indian Mutiny Rebellion against British rule in North India, 1857–59.

Jallianwala Bagh The enclosed ground in Amritsar where the massacre of Indian civilians took place in 1919.

Muslim League Organization founded in 1906 to promote the cause of Indian Muslims.

Partition The division of a country into separate parts, as India was divided into India and Pakistan in 1947.

Princely States The 570 states in India which were ruled by princes.

'Quit India' Movement An All-India, non-co-operation movement started by Congress in 1942 to force the British to leave India.

Raj The British Government of India, 1858–1947.

Round Table Conference An all-party conference held in London in 1931 to consider Dominion Status for India.

Royal Assent A Bill passed by both Houses of Parliament becomes Law only when signed by the Sovereign or the Royal Commissioners i.e. when given Royal Assent.

Satyāgraha Gandhi's doctrine of non-violent civil disobedience.

SEATO The South-East Asia Treaty Organization.

Tamil The language of southern India and of Tamil peoples in Sri Lanka.

Further reading

General Indian history
Majumdar, R. C. *et al. An Advanced History of India* (Macmillan, 1963)
Menon, V. P. *Transfer of Power* (Orient Longman, 1957)
Nehru, J. *India's Freedom – Essays, Letters and Speeches* (Unwin Books, 1965)
Philips, C. H. *et al. The Evolution of India and Pakistan 1858–1947. Select Documents* (Oxford University Press, 1962)
Poplai, S. L. (ed.) *Select Documents of Asian Affairs, 1947–50* (Oxford University Press, 1959)
Rawding, F. W. *The Rebellion in India, 1857* (Cambridge University Press, 1977)
Roberts, P. E. and Spear, T. H. P. *History of British India Under the Company and the Crown* (Oxford University Press, 1958)

Indian independence
Campbell – Johnson, A. *Mission with Mountbatten* (Robert Hale, 1951; reprinted Atheneum, New York, 1985)
Moon, P. (ed) *Wavell: The Viceroy's Journal* (Oxford University Press, 1973)
Pandey, B. N. *The Breakup of British India* (Macmillan, 1969)
Pandey, B. N. *The Rise of Modern India* (Hamish Hamilton, 1967)
Spear, P. *A History of India* Volume 2 (Penguin Books, 1970)

Pakistan
Feldman, H. *Revolution in Pakistan* (Oxford University Press, 1967)
Jalal, A. *The Sole Spokesman: Jinnah, the Muslim league and the Demand for Pakistan* (Cambridge University Press, 1985).
Tames, R. *India and Pakistan* (Batsford Educational, 1981)
Wheeler, R. S. *The Politics of Pakistan* (Cornell University Press, 1970)

Biography and autobiography
Mcdonough, S. *Mohammad Ali Jinnah, Maker of Modern Pakistan* (D. C. Heath, 1970)
Rawding, F. W. *Gandhi* (Cambridge University Press, 1980)

Index

Numbers that appear in **bold**
refer to the illustrations

All Jammu & Kashmir National
  Conference 59
Amritsar **16–17**, 150
  massacre of 25
Assam 34, 35, 39, 52,
  Provincial Congress Committee
  52
Attlee, Clement **33**, 35, 37, 38, 41
Awami League 67, 69

Baluchistan 41
Bangladesh 69, **71, 72**
Bengal 11, 32, 33, 34, 41, **45**, 50,
  52, 54
  partition of 24, 25, 38
Bhutto, Zulfikar Ali **66**, 67, 69, **70**
Bombay 10, 22, **27**, 34
Britain
  Empire 11, 20, 60
  Government 11, 20, 23, 33, 51
  Raj 17, 20, 23, 31, 41, 47

Calcutta **4–5, 8, 10**, 12, **14**, 37,
  41, 50, 52, **54, 55,** 57
Caste 13, 15
Cawnpore **20**
CENTO (The Baghdad Pact) 72
Clive of India 19
Churchill, Winston 51
Civil Disobedience Movement 29
Cripps, Sir Stafford 32, **35**

Dacca 65
Dalhousie, Lord 18
Delhi 35, 38, 41, 47, 48, **52,** 55
Direct Action Day **4–5, 8,** 9, **10,
  11,** 36, 37, 38
'Divide and Quit' 32
Dominion Status 29, 42, 51
Dyer, General 25

East India Company **18,** 19, 20
Elections
  India 27, 33
  Pakistan 66, 69

Gandhi, Indira **63**
Gandhi, Mahatma 11, 24, **25**, 27,
  28, 29, 30, 32, **40,**
  50, 55, **56,** 72
Gandhi, Rajiv **63**

Hindus 9, 10, 12, **12–13,** 28, 29,
  30, 36, 50, 53, 54
Hyderabad 44

India
  army 10, 23, **26**, 41, 59, 62
  civil service 22, 23, 41
  Constituent Assembly 48
  Constitution 56
  Food production **58**, 61, 62
  Independence 11, 20, 23, 24,
    28, 41, 42, 50, 59, 62
  National Congress 23, 24, 25,
    30, 31, 32, 33, 34, 36, 41,
    42, 52
  Pre-partition map **31**
  Post-partition map **41**
  Princely States 20, 40, 41, 42
  Self-rule 25, 26, 42
  United 11, 23, 29, 36, 40, 43
Instrument of Accession 43

Jinnah, Muhammad Ali **9**, 24, **25**
  27, 30, **31**, 32, **35**, 36, 37, **40**,
  41, 42, **45, 46, 47,** 57, 65

Kalistan 63
Khan, General Ayub **67**, 68
Khan, Liaquat Ali 30, **37**, 47, 57,
  64, 65
Karachi 34, 45
Kashmir **39**, 44, 55–59, 65

Lahore 50, 52
Legislative Assembly **43**, 48
Linlithgow, Lord 32, 39

Menon, V.P. 38, 40, 43
Montford reforms 26–27
Mountbatten, Lord **37, 38**, 39,
  40, 43, **46, 47**, 48, 51
Mujib, Sheikh **70**, 72
Muslims 15, 26, 32, 50, 53, 54,
  55, 70, 72
Muslim League 9, 11, 17, 24,
  30–31, 32, 33, 34, 42, 52, 65, 66,
  67
Muslim-Hindu-Sikh coalition 38
'Mutiny', Indian **20, 21**
Nehru **34, 36, 37**, 39, 40, **48, 49,
50, 52**, 56, 61
Non-violent civil disobedience **27,
28, 29**
North-West Frontier Province 27,
  30, 32, 34, 41

Pakistan 9, 10, 11, 24, 35, 36, 39,
  40, **41**, 42, 44, 47, 52, 55, 56,
  57, 59, 60, 63, 65, 69, 70, 72
  Anti-Pakistan Front 65, **68**
  Constituent Assembly 65–67
  Constitution 65, 67, 68
  East 52, 55, 57, 67, 69
  Food Crisis 65
  Islamic Republic 67
  People's Party 67, 69
  West 45, 57, 65

Patel, Vallabh-bhai **39**, 43, **48**, 56
Poverty 57, **71, 72**
Punjab 10, 15, 30, 32, 33, 34, 50,
  52, 54, 63
  East 35, 39, 41, 42
  West 41, 42, 52, 54

Queen Victoria 20, **22**
'Quit India' Movement 31, 32, 36

Refugees 52, **54, 55**, 56, **59**
Riots 28, **44**, 45, 62, 63
Round Table Conference **30**

Salt Laws, defiance of **28**–9
SEATO 72
Sikhs 10, 12, 15, **16–17**, 26, 40,
  41, 50, 52, 65
Simla conference 32
Sind 10, 27, 30, 32, 34, 41, 54

Transfer of power **46, 47**, 48, 52
'Tryst With Destiny' speech **49**

War
  First war of Independence **20,
21**
  India and Pakistan 56, **59**, 70
  West and East Pakistan 70
  World War I 25
  World War II 31
Wavell, Lord **11**, 32, 37, 39

Zia, General **69**

Picture Acknowledgements

Associated Press Ltd 50 (bottom); Camera Press Ltd 13 (top and
bottom), 16, 54, 60, 61, 66, 67, 69, 70, 72; Illustrated London News
cover; Peter Newark's Historical Pictures 18, 19, 26; Popperfoto
10, 12, 17, 20, 21, 25, 27, 28, 29, 30, 39, 46, 47, 52, 58, 62, 63, 64;
John Topham Picture Library 4–5, 8, 9, 11, 14, 22, 31, 33, 34, 35,
36, 37, 38, 40 (top and bottom) 42, 43, 44, 45, 48, 49, 50 (top),
51, 55, 56, 57, 59, 68;